YOUR LEGACY OF CARE

Providing for Your Special Needs Child Today, Tomorrow & Always

Donald Bailey
With J. William G. Chettle

Table of Contents

HEAVEN'S VERY SPECIAL CHILD

A meeting was held quite far from Earth!
"It's time again for another birth,"
Said the Angels to the LORD above,
This Special Child will need much love.

His progress may be very slow,
Accomplishments he may not show.
And he'll require extra care
From the folks he meets down there.

He may not run or laugh or play,
His thoughts may seem quite far away,
In many ways he won't adapt,
And he'll be known as handicapped.

So let's be careful where he's sent,
We want his life to be content.
Please LORD, find the parents who
Will do a special job for you.

They will not realize right away
The leading role they're asked to play,
But with this child sent from above
Comes stronger faith and richer love.

And soon they'll know the privilege given
In caring for their gift from Heaven.
Their precious charge, so meek and mild,
Is HEAVEN'S VERY SPECIAL CHILD.

by Edna Massionilla

Advance Praise for *Your Legacy of Care*

"As a lawyer, I know firsthand how important it is to plan. It takes discipline to put a life plan in place, but doing so saves time and money and minimizes the chances of emotional trauma. *Your Legacy of Care* is a beautifully written, practical roadmap to meet the myriad challenges of providing appropriate and sustainable care for a special needs family member. I commend the authors for sharing their expertise, experience, and wisdom to make the path smoother for all who face these challenges."

– William Hubbard
Partner, Nelson Mullins, Riley &
Scarborough LLP and National Bar Leader

"Typical financial advice is centered on parents who support children through college but no longer. Yet children with disabilities need support long after their parents are gone. Donald Bailey and William Chettle provide an excellent guide to plans that assure such children of support throughout their lives."

– Meir Statman
Glenn Klimek Professor of Finance, Santa Clara University

"Parents of children with special needs and disabilities will find *Your*

Legacy of Care most beneficial. Author Don Bailey's perspective as a parent, financial planner and former university board of trustees member is especially insightful. He includes supportive anecdotal passages from other parents and relates these to specific advice or resources that he has also found helpful. Mr. Bailey's inclusion of the Letter of Care provides not only a repository for important information about the special needs or disabled individual and their family, but also a 'living' document that includes such valuable information as behavioral concerns, favorite books, hobbies, fears and goals of the individual. As these particular items change, the Letter of Care can easily be amended. I applaud the efforts of Don Bailey and William Chettle. This helpful book, with its thoughtful checklist, will ensure that loved ones are provided for now and in the future."

– Dr. Harris Pastides
President, University of South Carolina

"It has been a privilege to know Donald Bailey and to see firsthand the results of his resolute work to expand post-secondary opportunities for individuals with intellectual and developmental disabilities. From its inception, the College Transition Connection has steadfastly supported the philosophy that, with the right supports, meaningful education and employment opportunities are not only possible, but essential for all individuals with the desire to pursue these options.

With *Your Legacy of Care*, Donald has masterfully blended the personal and professional aspects of his life experiences. He has brought into focus additional critical issues facing many families: the need for adequate resources and long-term planning. Speaking from his unique perspective and utilizing his expertise in the financial planning field, he has taken what many families and parents feel to be an intimidating and confusing set of hurdles and has framed an approach to addressing those in an easy-to-understand, step-wise guide to facing the realities of life care planning.

In both my professional and personal experiences, I have seen the painful struggle of families dealing with these issues: knowing what to do, when, and how. In this book, Donald has provided a thorough explanation of planning needs with accompanying resources and templates. He includes quotes and personal stories which capture the depth and emotion of making life decisions. I especially appreciate the joys of some of the experiences that are highlighted.

This book contains essential planning tools, and I look forward to families utilizing it in their life journeys."

– Barbara Hollis
Director of Vocational Rehabilitation in South Carolina (Ret.)

Foreword

As those of us who are parents of a child or adult child with a disability are aware, there are few more complex and unnerving responsibilities we face than fashioning a plan to address the needs of our family member for the short and long term.

On the one hand, this is an exciting time of new possibilities for individuals with disabilities in many dimensions of life — in education, employment, independent living and social inclusion. On the other hand, enabling them to take advantage of new possibilities through sound planning and resource management can seem daunting. Having an expert to guide one through a discussion of topics such as investments, estate planning, tax strategies, wealth protection and preservation is invaluable.

Author Donald Bailey, who is such an expert, has produced a book, *Your Legacy of Care: Providing for Your Special Needs Child Today, Tomorrow and Always*, that will contribute mightily to assisting those who seek to help improve the quality of life of individuals with disabilities now and in the future.

His first well-received book, *LIFE Learning is for Everyone*, details Bailey's very strategic and effective effort to spearhead the creation of postsecondary education programs at five top colleges and universities in South Carolina for students like his son who have an intellectual disability. In a significant pioneering achievement, Bailey was able to help secure funds from South Carolina's legislature to support the creation and expansion of these programs and, ultimately, to establish a scholarship fund for students who enroll in them.

Fully aware of the resource-intensive demands of supporting a family member with a disability not only through college but also across their lifespan, Bailey has written this second book. *Your Legacy of Care* is a natural outgrowth of his life experience as both the father of a son with special needs and a successful financial planner who founded his own firm and subsequently worked with countless numbers of clients to draw up estate and retirement plans. Bailey and his co-author William Chettle, also with many years of experience in financial services, have developed an excellent framework to follow in thinking about and planning for the lifelong requirements of a family member with a disability.

Well-organized and comprehensive, this book actually succeeds in demystifying the planning process by suggesting what questions to ask, what factors to consider for prioritization, and what steps to take. Compelling vignettes highlight the kinds of concerns and issues that individual parents and families grapple with as they move along on the path to build a plan for a loved one.

New and current information and resources provided in the book keep up with the latest developments in the field. The chapter on education discusses the growing number of post-secondary education programs available to students with intellectual disabilities across the country and the fact that certain types of financial aid may be available to them at individual institutions of higher education.

The chapter on education contains a coherent, understandable explanation of a groundbreaking change in federal tax law passed by Congress — the Achieving A Better Life Experience Act (ABLE) of 2014, which permits individuals with a disability and their parents and families to establish a tax-advantaged savings account to be used for education, health care, employment training and supports, housing and transportation expenses. The user-friendly self-assessment tool for individuals with a disability and their parents, and a model Letter of Care — a road map intended to provide detailed information and instruction regarding a loved one's personal, medical, legal, and financial needs — are generous gifts that will bring much-appreciated peace of mind to readers.

– Madeleine Will
Vice President, National Down Syndrome Society's Policy Center & Former Assistant Secretary of Special Education, U.S. Department of Education

Introduction

"We know that equality of individual ability has never existed and never will, but we do insist that equality of opportunity still must be sought."

– Franklin D. Roosevelt

As I sat in the airport lounge with my wife, about to embark on a long-planned, long-dreamed-of vacation to Paris, all I could think about was our son.

He was in his late twenties, living independently, doing remarkably well for a special needs adult, but would he be all right while we were away? Could we really leave him alone for an entire week — five time zones and an ocean away?

I looked over at my wife. She knew immediately what I was thinking.

"He'll be fine, Donald," she said. "I know he will be just fine. We've taken care of every possible detail."

Intellectually, I knew she was right. We had taken care of everything we could think of, arranging for friends and family and caregivers to be on call and to check in on him regularly.

But underneath our worries about this trip were the deeper worries that never seem to go away.

A week was nothing compared to the larger, often daunting challenge of making sure that our son would be taken care of for the rest of his life, especially after we were no longer around to help provide for him.

Many families with a member who has a disability feel like they are living on a very remote and lonely island. Families, friends and neighbors certainly are interested and willing to help, but they seldom understand the real impact special needs children can have on the dynamics of everyday living. They don't appreciate the sometimes overwhelming trials and tribulations. There are few breaks from responsibility, and the worries usually don't go away.

Of course, there are different levels of disabilities and many different needs, but most individuals with a disability will need some kind of lifetime care. That might mean someone who checks in from time to time or residential living or full-time, around-the-clock care. And all three of these options might be necessary at different times in your child's life.

And this leads to the biggest challenge of them all — protecting and caring for your family member when you are no longer around.

Depending on your child's level of disability, there are "homes" available that offer services, and many provide wonderful opportunities for friendship, care and support. But many families want their son or daughter to live independently as much as possible. Whatever decision is right for your child and your family, the big question remains: "How do we prepare financially for our child's life expectancy?"

The Facts on Special Needs and Disabilities

- Almost a third of families in the United States have at least one family member with a disability

- Nearly one-fifth of all Americans — more than 56 million men, women and children — have a physical, sensory, or intellectual disability and 38.3 million have a severe disability (source: U.S. Census 2010)

  o 14.9 million have a sensory disability involving sight or hearing

  o 20.1 million have a disability that limits their ability to engage in basic physical activity such as walking, climbing stairs, reaching, lifting or carrying

  o 15.1 million have a physical, mental or emotional condition that makes it difficult to learn, remember or concentrate

  o 9.4 million have a physical, mental or emotional condition that makes it difficult to dress, bathe or get around inside the home

  o 15.5 million have a disability that makes the activities of daily living — such as venturing outside the home, managing money or preparing meals — difficult

- The cost of raising a child to the age of 17 is around $234,000; that number can quadruple for a child with special needs, including costs such as:

- Occupational Therapy: $5,000 to $10,000
- Behavioral Therapy: $10,000
- Life Skills Therapy: $4,000
- Private Schooling: Up to $20,000
- Private Caregiver: $9,000

- 28.6 percent of people aged 15 to 64 with severe disabilities live in poverty, while 17.9 percent of adults with non-severe disabilities and 14.3 percent of people with no disability live in poverty

- Parents spend an average of $326 per month, or just under $4,000 per year, on out-of-pocket medical expenses on their special needs child

- Of the 62.2 million children under the age of 15, about 5.2 million or 8.4 percent have some kind of disability

- The probability of severe disability is one in 20 for people aged 15 to 24 and one in four for those aged 65 to 69

- People with disabilities constitute the nation's largest minority group and the only group any of us can become a member of at any time

Sources: U.S. Census Bureau; National Organization on Disability; www.fatherly. com/love-and-money/work-money/the-finacial-costs-of-raising-a-child-with-special-needs; www.lowcountrylawofc.com

****

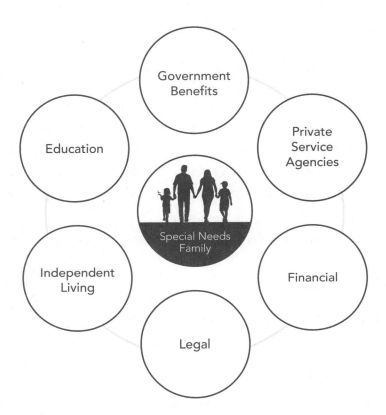

An Integrated Approach

As the diagram above shows, there are a number of factors and institutions that can play a significant role in your special needs journey.

Some of these — such as government benefits or legal considerations — can be so confusing, even overwhelming, that you are tempted to ignore them and try to get by as best you can.

But in my experience, taking an integrated approach — making the most of available resources and planning across your child's spectrum of needs and opportunities — gives you the highest probability of success.

Given some of the challenges you may face, this is absolutely crucial.

As a financial advisor, I spent my career helping my clients plan for and enjoy retirement. Usually that meant looking ahead three to four decades.

Though we couldn't know the future with anything approaching certainty, we could still make reasonable assumptions about longevity, spending, inflation and come up with a pretty good plan — one that my clients could adjust along the way as circumstances changed. While I handled the investments and the financial planning, I was generally confident that my clients could manage the rest of their lives.

With special needs children, however, you have to think about everything — guardians, retirement homes, insurance, even funeral arrangements. Then you need to figure out how it will all be paid for long after you have passed on from this world.

It is hard enough for the average family to save, invest and prepare for their own retirement. But with a special needs child, you are looking at stretching those funds you have worked for and saved to last not only through Mom and Dad's life expectancy, but perhaps another 30 years afterward as well.

As of this writing, I am in my late sixties, and my wife is...well, let's not go there, and just say she is many years younger. But for planning purposes, we assume that each of us will probably live another 20-25 years.

We both have worked all of our lives and have been fortunate to accumulate a fair amount in our retirement accounts. We have put a sound plan in place that should provide a comfortable income for us throughout retirement and make sure our son is taken care of for the rest of his life and will not be a burden on our daughter and her family.

Nothing in life is certain, but I feel reasonably confident that my wife and I, as well as our son <u>and</u> daughter, will be okay.

Even though I am an experienced financial advisor who does planning for a living, getting here wasn't always easy. I made a lot of mistakes along the way. But I also learned valuable lessons that I believe can help guide families in similar circumstances…and save them from many of the mistakes I made.

And that is what prompted me to write this book.

All kids are special and have special needs, but this book is for the parents of those children who will need some extra planning and support to live as an adult.

What follows is a step-by-step guide to putting together a lifetime plan for your family member. We'll look at everything from education to insurance to legal documents to investments to making sure your wishes for your child are carried out for the rest of his or her life.

Along the way, you may face countless issues and roadblocks. But with the right support, guidance and planning, your journey doesn't have to be a burden. It can provide you with peace of mind and confidence in the future.

Taking the First Step with Planning

"A goal without a plan is just a wish."

– Antoine de Saint-Exupéry

Having over four decades of experience in the investment advisory field, I understand the value of planning. I have helped many families prepare for their retirement and have witnessed firsthand the value of proper planning.

The intricacies of building a plan that takes into account investments, estate planning, tax strategies, wealth protection and preservation and other components can make coordinating your financial life a difficult job.

This is why most of us may need a team of financial professionals who will work in concert to make sure all aspects of our financial lives are being addressed. This becomes even more important when you have a special needs child.

Having your own team of experts working closely together helps maximize the effectiveness of your plan and makes sure it stays in sync with you and your child's current and future needs, with every item properly addressed. Your expert team will also help give you the highest probability of successfully achieving your own financial goals — which in turn gives you the highest probability of being able to provide a lifetime of care for your special needs child.

Your Special Needs Expert Team

Most of us need an accountant or CPA to (at minimum) do our taxes annually. If you have a good tax advisor, he or she can also be instrumental in the planning process by working hand in hand with other advisors to help avoid potential tax issues.

Almost everyone, and certainly high-net-worth individuals, should have a qualified tax attorney to review estate tax issues as well as recommend trust, family partnerships and investments that offer tax incentives. Working with your accountant, your tax attorney can help you avoid potential problems and help you navigate the advantages and disadvantages before you jump into an investment that sounds too good to be true.

At the very least, a tax attorney can help you create a will that will allow you to distribute your estate in accordance with your wishes. In the case of families who have a member with a disability, a special needs trust may be an essential instrument in making sure your loved ones are eligible for government services.

You should employ as a member of your team an attorney who is qualified and has experience working in the disability field.

Insurance advisors are important, and sometimes overlooked, members of your team. Not only should you typically have car insurance, health insurance, homeowner's insurance, disability and liability coverage, you probably need an umbrella policy, maybe rental insurance (if you have a rental or second home that your family member is living in), flood insurance (if you live on or near the water), even boat or art insurance. And of course, you should have disability and life insurance.

While all of these are important, life insurance can play a significant role in making sure there is plenty of money left for your child to help him/her live a comfortable and secure life. A male age 60 can purchase a $200,000 universal life policy for about $4,000 annually. A 40-year-old male can get the same death benefit for closer to $2,000 annually. Term insurance can be purchased for even less, at least initially, though it may be cost prohibitive as you get older. And a second-to-die policy, which typically is written on the life of Mom and Dad, is another option.

Buying insurance and making sure the beneficiary designation is set up to take advantage of the tax laws is critical. For your child, you probably need the proceeds to be placed in an irrevocable or special needs trust. Your attorney can help you make the proper decision. So start planning early; it may save you many thousands of dollars over your lifetime.

As a hedge against the rising cost of health insurance, it may also be prudent to evaluate the benefits of long-term care insurance. A 59-year-old woman can purchase a good long-term care policy for about $3,000 per year. This could provide as much as $150 per day in facility care or in-home benefits for up to three years. In South Carolina, where I live, the median annual cost of a nursing home semi-private room is almost $70,000. It won't take long to make a significant impact on your nest egg should you need prolonged assistance.

The unknown future cost of health care is a real cause for concern for many families. As one insurance agent I know suggests:

> "Many people who need long-term care insurance are those who could easily run out of money paying for care. On the other hand, for higher-net-worth individuals, the question boils down to how smart is it not to write a check for $4,000 each year to fund long-term care if you can afford to? Otherwise, their family members may have to write checks for $8,000 (or more) each month to pay bills for care, perhaps for several years. That makes no sense at all...especially when you realize that each month of

benefits that you receive is worth more than your insurance costs for a whole year. In other words, you typically could get back in benefits 12 times what you put in. 'Self-insuring' may seem like a smart idea until you start writing checks for long-term care. I have a client paying $16,000/month for high-quality home care. The numbers can get alarming! For a fraction of the interest some people are earning, they can transfer a good portion of the risk to an insurance company. Just because they may be able to self-insure doesn't mean they should."

I think long-term care insurance is not just about the financial costs. What happens when a spouse requires care and there is also a special needs child? When a friend of mine applied for a policy a few years ago, his wife was against the idea. But he told her, "If I need care, will you care for me or for our son first?" I think you know the answer..."

A hands-on caregiver will not have sufficient energy/resources to be a caregiver for a spouse and care or advocate for the child as well.

Health savings accounts (HSAs) also provide an opportunity to accumulate money on a tax-free basis, which can be used to help pay medical expenses. If your company has an HSA, you should contribute as much as allowed, or at least what you can afford. Remember, your contributions to the account are made in pretax dollars.

Not only can an experienced financial advisor be instrumental in helping you manage your money, he or she can often provide more comprehensive advice and planning (what is often referred to as wealth management). Your financial advisor should be able to work closely with all of the other advisors on your team of experts, bring them together and help make sure everyone is working in close alignment to determine the most beneficial course of action and strategy for all of your financial needs and goals — and your child's.

To give you the highest probability of success over the next 30 or 40 years, it is essential to have the right investment allocation for your goals and comfort with risk, regularly monitor how your portfolio and plan are performing, and make any adjustments as needed along the way.

Not only can a good financial advisor help you make the right decisions about your money, he or she should be able to take the lead role — in close partnership with other financial experts — in helping you navigate through all of the investment, legal, tax and insurance issues you will face as you plan for your life as well as for your special needs child.

Families with a member who has a disability also have to consider guardians and conservators, as well as therapists, doctors and adult service agencies, as part of the team. While financial advisors are not necessarily trained in these areas, if you happen to find an advisor who has a person with a disability in his or her family, he or she will certainly be more understanding of your needs and concerns.

Finding the right financial advisor and assembling a team of experts in these areas (and others) I've outlined will be critical to navigating through all of the issues you face. The expertise and experience required mean you should definitely <u>not</u> try to do this on your own. Don't be afraid to ask all of your advisors to meet together at least annually to review how you are doing. They are your team, dedicated to helping you and your child get where you want to go. And after all, you are paying them to help with your planning.

Self-Assessment

How well prepared are you for your child's future? How much planning have you done to date? What have you taken care of already? And what areas need more attention?

The following Self-Assessment is meant to help you better understand your unique circumstances, evaluate your situation and analyze the types of support and guidance you and your family may need. These questions cover the major areas you will need to address for your child.

While everyone's situation is different, ultimately most families will need to answer "Yes" to most of these questions. If you have a lot of "No" answers, don't feel bad. You now have a starting roadmap for the areas you will need to address.

Housing and Transportation

Do you have a clear vision of how you wish for your child/dependent to live when you are no longer around?	☐ Yes	☐ No
Do you know what housing options are available to your child/dependent in your state?	☐ Yes	☐ No
Is your child/dependent able to drive?	☐ Yes	☐ No
If your child/dependent is unable to drive, are you aware of the transportation options available to you in your state?	☐ Yes	☐ No
Other:	☐ Yes	☐ No

Education

When your child/dependent with special needs is 18, will he/she be able to function independently as an adult?	☐ Yes	☐ No
If not, would you apply for partial or full guardianship?	☐ Yes	☐ No
If your child/dependent is over 18, have you applied for guardianship?	☐ Yes	☐ No
Will your child's siblings be responsible for his/her care?	☐ Yes	☐ No
Other:	☐ Yes	☐ No

Government Benefits

Does your child/dependent own assets with a value greater than $2,000?	☐ Yes	☐ No
Do you have a complete understanding of the government benefits that your child/dependent is entitled to now and in the future?	☐ Yes	☐ No
Does your child/dependent have a representative payee appointed by Social Security?	☐ Yes	☐ No
Other:	☐ Yes	☐ No

Legal

Have you prepared a special needs or other trust for your child/dependent with special needs?	☐ Yes ☐ No
Does your child/dependent have a guardian?	☐ Yes ☐ No
Is a successor guardian named for your child/dependent?	☐ Yes ☐ No
Other:	☐ Yes ☐ No

Financial

Have you determined who will be financially responsible for your child/dependent with special needs?	☐ Yes ☐ No
Do you know what your child/dependent's monthly costs of living are?	☐ Yes ☐ No
Have you made any decisions on how to fund your child/dependent's trust?	☐ Yes ☐ No
Have you determined your retirement income needs?	☐ Yes ☐ No
Do you have insurance?	☐ Yes ☐ No
Have you determined the lifetime income needs of your child/dependent with special needs?	☐ Yes ☐ No
Other:	☐ Yes ☐ No

Employment/Recreation

Does your child/dependent currently work?	☐ Yes ☐ No
If not, would you like to understand the employment resources available to your child/dependent?	☐ Yes ☐ No
Does your child have an active social life with his/her peers?	☐ Yes ☐ No
Are you content with your child/dependent's social life?	☐ Yes ☐ No
Other:	☐ Yes ☐ No

Gwen's Journey

I am currently 55 years old and have four children: Miles, who recently graduated from Clemson and is looking for a job; Robin, currently attending Clemson; and identical twin daughters Wesley and M.E. (Mary Elizabeth), juniors at Beaufort High School.

During my third pregnancy, at 32 weeks, the doctors discovered I was having twin girls. Even though the ultrasound looked fine and I was told the girls looked healthy, that turned out to be anything but the case.

At their two-week checkup, we were told to see a geneticist, as the twins did not look "normal." Once we with met with the doctor, he informed us that the girls had a rare genetic disorder named Pfeiffer's syndrome. To this day, the girls are the only known identical twins born with Pfeiffer's syndrome. A month after their birth, the girls began what would be more than 50+ rounds of surgery. We liquidated our family farming business, and after 28 years of marriage, got divorced.

After we sold the farm, I began working as a media center assistant at the high school, which meant my income diminished dramatically.

What keeps me up at night? What doesn't keep me up?

I worry about my sons. Will they be productive men, good husbands? How can I comfort the girls when they are not asked to the prom, or any of the other activities that go along with the prom?

Will the girls be able to attend college? And how will I pay for college?

Will they survive the next surgery? How will I continue to pay for all their surgeries? What would happen to them should I die or lose my job? Am I a terrible mother? What can I do to advance my career so I can better provide for my family?

Will I ever get married again? Or for that matter, have a date? Ha ha.

Yikes, I am worse than I thought!

What worries me the most as it relates to my family is that there is not one person, related or nonrelated, whom I would trust to leave guardianship of my twins. Unfortunately, the girls never visit their dad more than a few hours at a time, and my sons are too young and too irresponsible to take guardianship.

Wesley plans on going to college to become a nutritionist. Hopefully we can make that happen with all her special needs. M.E. wanted to go to school to become a dental hygienist, hair stylist, or physical therapy assistant; however, because both of her elbows are fused, that would be virtually impossible.

I have not set up a trust for the girls yet, though I have spoken to an attorney. After being married for so many years, the divorce was very draining and expensive. Poor excuse, I know.

I also do not have a current will. I know I need to update it, because my husband is still the beneficiary. However, I do not believe my sons are mature enough to look after themselves. They need to show me that they are responsible with their money and have jobs.

My hope is that the girls will be able to live together alone once they are of age. Currently, they are working on getting their driver's licenses, though their fused elbows and fused vertebra make driving more complicated.

Neither girl currently has a job, but they occasionally dog sit. They also love to babysit, but are rarely asked. Because of several physical issues, Wesley has a hard time standing or walking for any length of time and tires easily.

At this time, I cannot think 50 days ahead, never mind 50 years ahead. I am still working toward trying to live within my means, as the girls have so many medical expenses. My ex-husband does not help much, as he has not worked in more than six years.

Several years ago, when I was referred to an attorney regarding Social Security, he told me that the twins did not qualify because of my assets — I own four acres on the water. I do not plan to sell the land, as it has been in my former husband's family for generations, and I want to leave it to my children. I plan to contact the Social Security office to see if they would qualify when they turn 18. The girls currently have TEFRA Medicaid.

I have a financial advisor who is helping me; however, his plan does not include helping my children with college tuition. But I continue to help my son pay for college, so my finances are dwindling.

Education

We all know that education costs are soaring. According to the College Board, the average cost of tuition and fees for the 2016–2017 school years was $33,480 at private colleges and $9,650 for state residents at public colleges ($24,930 for out-of-state residents). Factor in room and board and inflation, and the average cost of a four-year public college education today could be around $70,000. In 18 years, that cost is projected to be more than $150,000.

Before they can even think about college, families with special needs children often incur major educational expenses.

We spent in excess of $500,000 for our son's education, and we sometimes wonder if it was worth it. In the first grade at our local public grammar school, we were told they could not help our son! The principal said, "We do not have the tools that he needs to be successful."

Were we angry?

I can't say we were happy, but at least someone was being honest with us. So we searched and found a local private school that our son attended for the next five-and-a-half years until the day the headmaster called us in and told us our son had hit a wall, and they didn't think he should continue his education there.

After trying public middle school for one semester, it was clear that our son was not getting out of it what we had hoped he would, so we found an out-of-state private school for him. He spent the next two-and-a-half years there before finally coming back home and attending his hometown public high school.

He did fine. After a long, and at times difficult, educational journey, he'd finally completed his K – 12 years.

Current law allows special needs students to stay in high school until age 21. And some states allow the student to receive services until they turn 22, or in Michigan, until age 26.

I am sure the experts who came up with this extended "education" for our children think it is an opportunity to help, but from my perspective, it often means nothing more than an extended day care service.

Most families I have spoken with agree that the extended time doesn't accomplish much, educationally speaking. So while many typical high school graduates go on to college, our special needs kids stay in high school.

You might ask, why do kids with special needs even want to go to college?

The best way to answer this question is to ask why any young person wants to attend college: freedom, independence, expanded knowledge, late-night pizza, lifelong new friends and even the opportunity to learn. Well, guess what? Kids with special needs also want to have the same kinds of experiences.

There is a movement around the country, and internationally, to allow young people who have an intellectual disability to attend college. Currently, there are over 200 post-secondary opportunities in the U.S., and they are growing every year. In South Carolina, we are fortunate to have five colleges that offer special needs kids the chance to attend college. Some of these are two-year programs, while some include four-year options. The requirements at each school may vary, but all prospective students have to apply (just like typical students) and go through an admissions process before they are admitted. Some of the admission requirements are:

- The student must have an intellectual disability

- Must have a desire to attend college

- Must read on at least a fourth grade level

- Must be able to self-medicate

- Must possess functional communication skills

- Must have two references from non-family members

After the student is accepted, depending on the college, he/she will receive a customized plan based on his/her interest and needs. Some of the courses offered are philosophy, theater, art, physical education, computers, and time and money management. Most of these programs also provide internships for the students to get a taste of employment demands and the experience that comes with job responsibilities. Many of these classes are shared with traditional students. Inclusion is a win for everyone, the traditional student as well as the student with a disability.

The goals for special needs students are to continue learning, be employable, develop social skills, experience college and learn how to be independent — pretty much like your typical college kid.

Our son was fortunate to attend four years of college, one year out of state and three at our state university. College isn't cheap, but we wanted to give him every opportunity to grow, experience college life and have a full, meaningful, independent life.

These college programs typically are created on an audit basis, so these kids don't graduate with a degree, but they do get a certificate of completion. Many of the colleges do include these kids in graduation exercises along with everyone else. I can tell you from a personal perspective that we were extremely proud watching our son walk across that stage.

Though 529 plans (which are tax-advantaged savings plans operated by a state or educational institution designed to help families set aside funds for future college costs) are not available for these students, there is financial help available. In December 2014, President Obama signed the Stephen H. Beck Achieving a Better Life Experience Act (also known as the ABLE Act) into law, allowing families to create a tax-free savings account for young people who incur a serious disability prior to their 26th birthday — without the funds counting against federal benefits.

Under current gift-tax limitations, the total annual contributions by all participating individuals, including family and friends, is $14,000 per account, adjusted annually for inflation. The overall contribution limit for ABLE accounts is subject to individual state limits for education-related 529 savings accounts. Many states have set this limit at more than $300,000 per plan. However, for individuals with disabilities who are recipients of Supplemental Security Income and Medicaid, the first $100,000 in ABLE accounts is exempted from the SSI $2,000 individual resource limit. If the account exceeds $100,000, public benefits are not terminated, but rather suspended until the account level is reduced to $100,000 or below.

Similar to 529 accounts, interest earned on savings and withdrawals for authorized purposes is tax-free. Funds accrued in the accounts can be used to pay for education, health care, transportation, housing, employment training and support and many other expenses incurred across the lifespan of the person with a disability. Each person may only open one ABLE account.

While the law alters federal rules to allow for ABLE accounts, each state must now pass its own ABLE Act (if it chooses to do so) and put regulations in place — much as states have done for other types of 529 plans — so that financial institutions can make the new offering available. By the way, there is no obligation to use the ABLE account in your state of residency. A friend of mine in New Jersey set up his son's ABLE account with Tennessee (which has most of its investment options in passively managed and asset class options). Some states also have significantly lower (or higher) fees than others.

Pell Grants, Federal Supplemental Educational Opportunity Grants, and Federal Work-Study jobs are available in some but not all programs. Each college must apply for approval before the students can access these funds. The state of South Carolina was one of the first to offer a grant to families who meet the needs-based criteria.

All five programs in South Carolina have applied and qualify for students in their programs to receive federal financial aid, if the students and their families meet the financial eligibility guidelines. There are other pockets of funding available, but you have to do your homework to find those sources.

So do we think sending our son to college was worth it? Yes, we believe he grew as an individual and gained a lot of self-confidence. He learned how to take care of himself. He learned how to be independent, and he is living on his own, is happy, and is a productive member of society.

I would urge every parent to make college education a goal for their special needs child. This means you have to start planning at an early age, just as you would for any child. Because you may have to pay for additional education and your child will probably not be able to contribute significantly to his/her tuition, your costs will be higher. But as almost every parent I know who has sent their child to college will agree, the rewards will be truly meaningful.

Independence

"Disability is a matter of perception. If you can do just one thing well, you're needed by someone."

– Martina Navratilova

All parents want their children to grow up to be independent, productive members of society. We typically take for granted that they will leave home at some time in their early adulthood, get a job, buy (or at least rent) their own home, own a car, have a circle of friends and start taking care of themselves.

Parents are always concerned for their children's welfare, but for the most part, we push them out of the nest and allow them to fly on their own. Although parents, young parents in particular, are keenly focused on developing and nurturing self-determination skills in their child, a family member with a disability often requires ongoing support of one type or another. Of course, the level of the disability will have a major impact on the level of care and involvement parents will need to provide when their child is grown up.

Let's look at some of the major independent living issues our children will face in six key areas:

- Housing

- Transportation

- Health and Fitness

- Friends/Social Life

- Employment

- Everyday Living

Housing

Historically, housing for people with intellectual and developmental disabilities mainly consisted of forced institutionalization without consideration for the person's preference, hopes, dreams or quality of life.

Many young people with a disability end up staying at home with Mom and Dad. There are many reasons for this, beginning with cost. Many families may not have the financial resources to buy a home or even rent a place for their son or daughter to live on his/her own. In fact, over 700,000 families, many headed by individuals who themselves are aging, have a family member with a disability residing at home.

Remember, depending on the level of the disability, the cost will probably be the responsibility of Mom and Dad, and then of the estate after you are gone. Depending on where you live, the size of the home, the taxes and insurance, not to mention the upkeep, and of course, the mortgage, this could be a significant financial obligation for many years to come. Taxes, insurance and upkeep alone could be

$4,000 or $5,000 every year.

Renting a house is another option. Maybe your child could have a roommate and share the cost? Depending on where you live in the country, how big the house/apartment is, and what amenities it has, rent could easily run $1,000 – $2,000 a month. The cost to provide support can be much higher.

Group housing is an option that may be more affordable. It provides companionship, a level of independence and usually supervision. Most importantly, it does give parents a reprieve, as well as providing the young person with a feeling of independence from Mom and Dad.

Other options may include cluster housing with a small number of houses on the same site in close proximity to one another. This allows special needs individuals to live close to one another. Village communities are self-contained communities with services provided on site. Dispersed housing refers to a model of providing housing and independent living support within the community.

Often the decision on housing comes down to how much it is going to cost and whether there will be any governmental support. Unfortunately, public funds available for residential supports are insufficient to serve the large number of individuals currently on waiting lists for services.

Nationwide, the monies available do not keep up with the need we have to provide good, safe residential options. So parents often are left with paying the bill or keeping their now-adult child at home. But the questions remains, what happens after Mom and Dad are no longer here? That is why making housing decisions now, and planning for the future, after you are gone, is so important.

Transportation

If your son is living in his own house or apartment, now you have to think about transportation, especially if he has a job. How is he going to get to work and back? Can he drive? Does he have a driver's license?

Perhaps he lives on a bus line and can jump on and off with little help. This is a wonderful option when it works. For the most part, the costs are minimal. For those families who live in a larger metropolitan area, there could be a train or subway system that can provide a wonderful and reliable means of transportation. This does have its drawbacks, like when your child misses the bus or the bus breaks down. Travel training to assist your son or daughter in learning how to use public transportation may be available through a variety of sources. Paratransit is required under the Americans with Disabilities Act as an alternative for persons with disabilities who cannot use mass transit; however, significant problems exist with reliability and service.

And not everyone lives in a town or community that has an easily accessible mass transit system. Understanding the rules of public transportation can also be a challenge.

If you are in a smaller town, taking cabs or Uber might work, but the cost could become an issue depending on how far away work is and how many days per week transportation is needed. So maybe the answer is Mom, Dad, or perhaps a sibling?

Really...just think about that for a minute.

That is a disaster waiting to happen. First of all, Mom and Dad are not going to be around forever. And do you really want to put chauffeuring duties on a brother or sister?

Not all people who have a disability are incapable of driving. Some are very capable, and this certainly makes life easier for everyone and can give the individual a lot of freedom. However, this too can have significant cost. In addition to the cost of purchasing a car, its operation, maintenance, taxes and insurance represent another $2,000 to 3,000 per year. According to a 2014 study by AAA, driving 15,000 miles per year on average costs over $9,000 per year, depending on the type of car you drive. Some individuals with disabilities who are self-employed may purchase a business vehicle that is driven by another person.

Health and Fitness

Health is probably one of the biggest issues people with a disability have to come to terms with. Again, depending on the disability, staying fit and healthy can be a real challenge.

Or it may be hard for your child to understand the value of and need for regular physical activity (and too many Americans in general don't exercise enough or look after their health). There are opportunities for participation in unified sports programs that offer younger kids as well as teenagers and young adults a chance to be on a team and increase their physical activity. Special Olympics gives many people with all types of disabilities the chance to compete and improve their health by competing in local, regional and national events. In addition to physical health benefits, exercise can give an emotional boost of self-esteem. Just being a member of a team or winning a medal goes a long way in providing self-worth. An added benefit of team participation is the social connections that are made on the field or in the gym.

Hiring a trainer to help educate and coach your child is an option that has many benefits for him or her. It can be expensive, but if it helps your child stay healthy and in shape, it may end up saving you thousands of dollars in unwanted medical costs. Joe Ryan, Ph.D., and Daniel A. Traylor at Clemson University have recently written a book, *Promoting Healthy Lifestyles for Individuals with Intellectual Disabilities*, on health issues and ways in which people with disabilities can utilize various methods to improve their physical fitness.

Poor fitness can snowball into myriad health issues, from obesity to diabetes to heart issues. From a financial and planning perspective, bad health can become a major cost issue, with the potential to disrupt even the best-made plans.

Health insurance is not cheap, and I don't see costs coming down anytime soon under the current system. Teaching and preaching are all parents can do once a young person reaches his or her 20s. Even if your child is not living on her own, she certainly thinks she is and doesn't want to listen to Mom and Dad much. All we can really do is to continue to encourage and talk with our children about the benefits of staying healthy and fit.

Friends/Social Life

One of the hardest areas for some people who have a disability is feeling accepted. Unfortunately, in today's society, people with disabilities are sometimes treated as though they are different. As a result, they may have a difficult time making and keeping friends.

This is one of the most frustrating areas from a parent's perspective. Often, family members may be your child's only friends and means of having a social life.

In my experience, exposure to church and family functions, school reunions and all the things we all do to stay connected in day-to-day life can also help your child find connections and friends. It can be hard work, and you have to do most of it yourself.

However, if your child is able to work, a broader world of social connections and friendship becomes possible. People who have a disability often find that work provides them with fulfilling and engaging social interactions. They value the camaraderie the workplace can provide and the sense of purpose that comes from a team effort to accomplish common goals.

Dr. Cindi May, a professor at The College of Charleston, along with her team, has designed a website, tci.cofc.edu/index.html, that is a wonderful resource for helping your child navigate social opportunities online. The site is simple, easy to use and provides pointers for your child on social media. Some people with an intellectual disability may need additional help in learning how to use the internet and, of course, should be taught about the potential pitfalls that come with it.

Employment

We are witnessing a welcome change in the workplace as many companies become increasingly open to hiring people with disabilities, but we still have a long way to go.

People with disabilities have proven over and over again that they have the ability to perform many jobs as well as the next guy or gal. As a matter of fact, there are many advantageous reasons why employers like to hire from the disabled community. Individuals with disabilities are competent workers who are capable of mastering many tasks associated with a multiplicity of jobs and careers, particularly if their interests and abilities have been matched to a specific position or "bundle" of tasks through processes known as "discovery" and person-centered planning. Additionally, they are generally on time, don't miss work, don't have drinking issues or drug problems, and they are glad to be on the job. The bottom line is they are often remarkably dependable and get on well with their fellow workers and customers. There are also some tax incentives for employers to hire disabled employees for full- and part-time jobs and paid internships/apprenticeships. An experimental project in Salt Lake City, Utah, provides a FICA tax reduction to employers who offer paid apprenticeships. Dollars saved by the employers are then utilized for supports for the individual with a disability.

Unfortunately, there still may be not enough employers hiring, and consequently, the unemployment rates for people with a disability remain high. Most states, through their departments of vocational rehabilitation, offer employment training and will help in job placements.

Everyday Living

Most of us breeze through our days with little difficulty. We do a hundred different things without thinking or realizing how difficult some of them might be for others.

But managing ordinary life for members of the disabled community can often be a real challenge and in some cases may mean additional expenses that must be included in long-term planning.

Can your child pay bills? Or does he or she need to have someone take on that responsibility every month?

Can he or she go to the store and keep food and everyday necessities in the house? Or is a part-time helper needed for this chore?

Getting haircuts, going to the doctor and the dentist, keeping the yard cut and clean, maintenance of the property…these all can be difficult for a person with a disability to do without assistance. That means you may have to pay someone to help make sure these things are done on a regular basis.

We can't forget the challenges of not only grocery shopping, but also preparing food and maintaining a good, balanced diet. This can be a major issue.

Learning and understanding the importance of eating properly has huge implications on future health and expenses for all of us. Those with intellectual disabilities often don't understand the effect of not eating properly and consequently don't understand the importance of purchasing healthy, nutritional food. In fact, they may tend to purchase foods that are not healthy and often are more expensive. Again, the long-term implications for the cost of health care can be significant.

If you add up all the costs of caring for your child day to day and year to year, you can get to a big number all too quickly.

The long-term rate of inflation in the U.S. is around three percent a year. That means prices, on average, double every 34 years. So a child in his early 20s will need twice as much to live on when he reaches his late 40s and twice that again in his 70s. These numbers clearly indicate the need to plan for what happens if Mom and Dad are suddenly gone.

And some costs, such as education and health care, have historically grown significantly faster than three percent.

Depending on your child's level of disability, this can have a significant impact on planning and budgeting for the future.

Before you throw up your hands in surrender, remember that we are simply trying to show you the potential needs so you will have a more comprehensive perspective on why it is so important to make sure your son or daughter is protected, at least from a financial planning perspective.

****

For more research and information on these and other independent living topics, visit www.collegetransitionconnection.org.

Mindy's Journey

My son received an autism diagnosis at age 2. The day I got the diagnosis, I saw a group of boys riding bikes, and I thought, "My son will never have friends." I almost collapsed on the floor.

After we got the diagnosis, we left the doctor's office with nothing, just a sheet of paper filled with jargon. We went home and told our family and relatives, and we got a terrible response from some of them. That was almost as debilitating as the diagnosis.

I soon found myself struggling to identify the resources we'd need. It was a real ordeal just trying to find basic services and support. Mostly, people were helpful, but there was no central place I could go to get the information I needed. So I had to piece everything together.

Later, we found out that my son had lead poisoning from all the renovation work we were doing on our historic home. He was treated, and the same agency reversed his diagnosis at age 5. And that day I promised myself, "I'm going to do something. I'm going to pay it forward." Starting from our family's experience, my vision of what was possible became bigger because I saw other needs to address.

Today, our son is doing great, developing typically, playing all-star sports, and enjoying friendships. In some ways, it's like the lead poisoning never happened. But our experience led me to help found Special Family Resource, a nonprofit network dedicated to bridging gaps between special needs organizations, providers and families. Our local providers are busy; they're providing services, and often, they just don't know what resources are available. So we hope that parents can be pointed to resources through us instead of having to do all the research themselves. Special Family Resource is focused on Mom, Dad, siblings, so that providers can concentrate on individuals with special needs. We ask, "What can we do for the family?"

And the main thing that we do is provide a network. There are a lot of great resources, yet when I talk to program directors, a lot of times they are unaware of resources just down the street! It's unreal.

So accessibility is key. It's about families building friendships. That gets the parents out of isolation, and then they can fight the depression that many special needs families face because they are so isolated. This is a hopeful way to deal with any diagnosis…it's about getting people into those networks so they can receive support.

It's overwhelming to think what good could come out of this resource. Once we begin collaboration, incredible things can happen.

Trusts, Wills & Other Legal Documents

"Let's stop 'tolerating' or 'accepting' difference, as if we're so much better for not being different in the first place. Instead, let's celebrate difference, because in this world it takes a lot of guts to be different."

– Kate Bornstein

The size of your estate will dictate the types of legal documents you need, but, shockingly, 61 percent of Americans — as well as 70 percent of those with children under age 18 — do not even have a will.[1] A will helps ensure that your money, possessions and property go to the people and organizations you care about most. This is particularly important when you factor in caring for your child across the full span of his/her life.

In addition to a will, a basic estate plan should also address what would happen to your affairs if you are no longer able to act on your own behalf. To this end, you should consider having a living will, a durable power of attorney for health care and possibly a general durable power of attorney as well.

Sometimes called an "advance directive," a living will details how you want to be cared for if you become incapacitated and unable to

---

[1] 2013 Harris Interactive Survey

communicate your wishes. Your living will can be as specific as you want about the kind of health care you wish to receive, including life support and other medical interventions such as feeding tubes and resuscitation.

Via a durable power of attorney for health care document, you appoint someone to make all necessary health care decisions for you and ensure that your health care providers act in accordance with your written wishes. This person should be someone you trust who, ideally, lives in close geographic proximity.

A durable power of attorney document specifies who will handle your affairs and financial decisions if you are unable to. This person should be detail-oriented and comfortable with financial matters.

With a family member who has a disability, everything becomes more complex.

Depending on the level of disability, you may need to have someone appointed as a guardian and/or a conservator or seek to obtain limited guardianship in areas such as medical decision making and financial management.

A guardian must, by law, act in the best interest of the individual (often called a ward) with a disability. It is the guardian's responsibility to report to the court at least annually, sometimes more often. It is the guardian's duty to handle health care and other decisions, while a conservator is charged with managing the ward's financial needs. A guardian may be appointed to make decisions for the person in some areas, but not others. For instance, the right to vote can be retained. This is known as Supported Decision Making, which is focused on empowering special needs individuals to be the ultimate decision makers in as many areas as possible while also providing the assistance they need to make decisions on their own. For more information, see www.supporteddecisionmaking.org.

When considering who will be the guardian for your child, it is important to focus the discussion on actual parenting (or adult parenting) abilities and willingness to do the job. What is not helpful is to get hung up on possibly hurting anyone's feelings or bypassing friends or family members who might expect to be guardians but aren't the best choice. Most importantly, a guardian should be willing and able to take care of your child if the need arises, so an essential step is to discuss the responsibilities with the potential guardian beforehand.

A special needs trust is one way to protect your son or daughter's assets while keeping them out of your child's name. This is done so your child will not be unjustly penalized or forfeit government benefits. A growing number of individuals with disabilities are eligible for both Supplemental Security Income (SSI) and Social Security Disability Insurance (SSDI). They become eligible because they are dependent adult children (DACs) and a parent has died or is retired and, therefore, the adult person with a disability becomes eligible for SSDI and, eventually, for Medicare. Other adults with disabilities who work and pay into Social Security Disability Insurance earn their way to SSDI eligibility. These persons are part of the population who are identified as "duly eligible" for SSI and SSDI.

As of this writing, individuals who have assets of more than $2,000 in their names can be disqualified from receiving Social Security benefits and Medicaid. This does not include monies invested as a result of the ABLE Act (see pages 36 – 37 for more information).

And once eligible for SSDI, the individual is no longer subject to the $2,000 asset limitation.

Special needs trusts are taxed at the highest possible rate. The applicable tax rate, though, depends on how the trust is structured and can vary greatly. It's important to work with a knowledgeable special needs attorney in order to minimize that liability.

ABLE accounts are tax advantaged; however, when the beneficiary with a disability passes away, the ABLE legislation requires that the Medicaid program be paid back for Medicaid funds received by the beneficiary. Special needs trusts do not require a payback, and funds remaining in a trust can be bequeathed to a non-disabled sibling or family member. Some well-off families with a disabled family member are seeking to utilize both a special needs trust and an ABLE account and see the two as complementary.

Another trust for you to consider is an insurance trust, which is set up to receive insurance proceeds on behalf of your child or young adult. It can be set up (assuming it is properly managed) so that your family member could receive the benefits for his or her lifetime, with the right to draw on principal in the case of emergencies.

Your insurance advisor and your tax attorney can work together to ensure that the trust is set up in a proper way to avoid taxes, with money being available when needed. If a family does not designate a family member as the trustee, it might be a good idea to designate a trusted family member as the "trust protector."

Having your wealth advisor working with all of your advisors to create a financial and estate plan will create a clearer path for your journey. If you put everything in writing and meet on a regular basis to review and tweak your plans based on your family needs and current situation, you will be in a sound position to provide for yourself as well as the next generation.

But in my opinion, one of the most important documents for guiding the care of your special needs child is a booklet of information our family has put together that we call a Letter of Care (also known as a Letter of Intent).

A Letter of Care is designed to help ease the emotional and financial burden associated with caring for a loved one with special needs. The steps you must take can be difficult. They may even make you, or your loved one, uncomfortable. But taking these steps can have a profound impact on the quality of your loved one's life after you are gone.

We have included a sample Letter of Care template as an appendix, starting on page 71.

The Letter of Care provides essential information about your loved one's personal, medical, legal, and financial needs to guardians, caregivers, relatives or friends — those responsible for providing physical, emotional and financial care when you no longer can. Like a map, it guides the caregivers through the day-to-day support your loved one requires.

Our Letter of Care is intended for our daughter to have. It includes pertinent personal information about our son, such as his doctors' names, Social Security number, driver's license number and expiration date, passwords, credit card numbers, banking account, and auto, homeowner's and health insurance, as well as a reminder of things that happen or needs to be taken care of every month, such as doctors' appointments, when bills are due, when the garbage should be taken out, when the car insurance is due. It also includes directions on our wishes should something untimely happen to us.

It has been a very interesting process trying to remember things that most of us take for granted — the everyday responsibilities we all carry out without a second thought.

More importantly, we included our hopes and desires in the Letter of Care so that others will know our wishes for the future and be able to carry them out.

The Letter of Care is meant to be a living document, something that you should revisit from time to time when information changes or when milestones are met. The Letter of Care is not a legal document, but it should be signed and dated upon completion. Any updates should also be signed and dated.

Once complete, please share your Letter of Care with the people who are most likely to provide care and have responsibility for your family member with special needs.

You should also place a copy with other important documents, such as your will.

Marilyn's Journey

I worry constantly that Janice will not have the resources or support she needs.

We are redoing our will and living trusts. Janice has a trust set up by her grandparents that is not a special needs trust. There is enough in the trust to be a help, but not to provide the resources she will need for the rest of her life.

Janice is very unlikely to be able to live alone, unless it was next door to someone providing support. She could probably live in a supported living arrangement, but it would have to be a situation where there was well-trained support with family oversight. Her medical situation is such that there is a need for supervision with her medications and taking her to frequent medical and physical therapy appointments. We actually have full guardianship for Janice. But we do believe in the importance of Supported Decision Making. So after much soul-searching, we decided that she would retain her right to vote. I think she is at least as perceptive as many other voters.

I spent two years working with a parent organization in our area, exploring living situations, visiting other states, doing a survey, etc., and have not yet figured out a good living situation for her where we live.

Her sister and family are moving to another state. We are considering moving there (probably in a couple of years) and working on setting up a living situation for Janice that could continue after we die, with her sister helping look after her. One option might be to buy a house near her sister and have a roommate and support person live in the house with her.

She did have a part-time job paying $12 an hour that she loved. But it didn't last. Now she is volunteering and taking community education classes, which she enjoys. But she has no income currently. When she did have paid work, it was enough (about $400 a month) to pay for her lunches, items she wanted to buy, like DVDs, gifts, etc., which was a help to our family budget, and more importantly, made her feel good.

The big equation for our family, as it is for so many others, is how much will be required for my husband and me to live on until we die, what expenses like long-term care may arise, etc. The other piece I am grappling with as we redo our wills and living trust is how to divide the money we are leaving among Janice and our other adult children.

She gets SSDI since my husband is retired (about $900 per month) but doesn't qualify for Medicaid because of the trust set up by her grandparents. She is on Medicare and has Blue Cross secondary insurance as a disabled adult child, since my husband is retired. However, one never knows how long that will continue.

I am not clear on what she will need in the future. If I could come up with a dollar amount that she will need for support for the rest of her life and how much my husband and I can reasonably plan on contributing to that number, it would help significantly with our planning and my peace of mind.

I really need to figure this out soon.

Planning & Investing for the Long Term

"If you want to go fast, go alone. If you want to go far, go together."

– African Proverb

Leaving aside education, we estimate that we will need to provide at least $25,000 a year for our son (adjusted for inflation) if something should happen to us in the near future. This number will certainly increase as he gets older.

To generate this kind of income with a reasonable probability of success means we would suggest a nest egg of a minimum of $500,000, with the expectation that it will grow over time before it is needed. This will guarantee (as much as possible) that our son will be taken care of financially and not become a ward of the state, or even worse, end up homeless.

If $500,000 sounds like a daunting number, it is.

However, there are a few things we can do to reduce this number.

First, apply for Social Security Disability Insurance (SSDI) and Supplemental Security Income (SSI) if your child qualifies. Depending on the nature and severity of the disability, Social Security and Medicare, Medicaid and a Medicaid Waiver can help reduce your child's immediate need. If your child receives SSDI and/ or SSI, be aware of the asset and income limitations for SSI and the income limitations for SSDI.

Second, look at your life insurance and update the amount to help create immediate liquidity in the event of your death. Depending on the age of the parents, it can be the least expensive assurance that you have enough money for your son or daughter to be taken care of for their lifetime. If you are looking to have $500,000 available for your child and you are 50 years old and in good health, you can buy a universal life policy for under $4,000 per year.

Of course, the older you are, the more expensive the coverage is. Think about it: you can leave a half a million dollars in trust, which could generate an income stream of $20,000 to $25,000 annually at a cost to you of no more than $ 4,000 per year.

If you are unsure about investing in stocks, you can have the proceeds placed in an annuity contract that will pay an income for the life of your dependent. By the time your child reaches 50, the annuity should pay a monthly income for life of approximately $2,200, depending on the company and the current rates at the time of death.

The problem with this option is that it makes no adjustments for inflation and if your dependent dies at an early age, the remaining balance goes to the company. The flip side is if your dependent lives a long, healthy life, she will receive those monthly checks for her lifetime. There are many other options with annuity contracts that you will want to review carefully with your financial advisor.

You don't have to buy a universal life policy, either — there are other types of insurance that may work better for your situation. Term insurance for younger families may be a better option, since the costs will be lower. Working with your financial advisor, insurance specialist, CPA and other professionals will make it much easier for you to make the right decision based on your needs, age and tax situation.

If you can afford to purchase an insurance policy, it will help reduce the need for accumulating the entire $500,000 before you pass.

My wife and I don't know how long we are going to live and don't know if our projections will be accurate, so we have enough life insurance to help support my wife (should I die unexpectedly) as well as our children. This part of the financial plan is really the same for any family.

It is also important to start investing with your future and your child's future in mind. While planning financially for your own life is a challenge, given the uncertainties of markets and the economy and how long you will live, it becomes even more complex when you try to factor in planning for another generation. This is why I believe it is so important to work with an experienced fee-based financial advisor.

As the name suggests, fee-based advisors charge clients a fee for their services and are therefore not compensated by commissions on sales of investments. As a result, fee-based advisors' interests are aligned with their clients' interests. That means a fee-based advisor is highly motivated to give you the best advice for your situation at all times — even if that advice is to sit tight and do nothing.

Based on my experience over the years, I also believe you should invest on a regular basis in a globally-diversified portfolio using a combination of low-cost, passively managed index or asset class funds. Your future — and your child's — are too important to have to depend on consistently outguessing the market, something even most experienced money managers are unable to do consistently or predictably.

You should also rebalance your portfolio regularly to help keep it aligned with your long-term plan.

We've all heard the investing adage that we should "buy low, sell high." This is exactly what rebalancing does, taking money from assets that have performed well and reinvesting in assets that haven't. Rebalancing does not guarantee greater returns over every period, but it helps reduce portfolio risk and may deliver better risk-adjusted returns over time. Remember, rebalancing does not guarantee a return or protect against a loss. The buying and selling of securities for the purpose of rebalancing may have adverse tax consequences.

As you get older, you should also consider being a little more conservative with your portfolio and not take as much risk. Obviously, you may not get the highest returns, but neither will you get hurt as badly in the down markets.

And believe me, there will be more down markets.

After 40 years of being in financial services, I have seen at least five major corrections, from the 500-point drop in one day in the 1980s to the bust of the technology industry in early 2000 to the most recent "Great Recession," when most markets were down 30% – 40%. They have all rebounded, and I believe that in the future they will continue to grow, despite some bumps along the way.

How you prepare for the "bumps" can have a big impact on your portfolio's returns.

Taking advantage of domestic and international, large and small, growth and value positions will afford you the opportunity to participate in all markets with not too much exposure to any one market.

Perhaps the most difficult decision is the proper allocation into each of these assets. Depending on your age and your child's age, these assets must last for a long time. The dilemma is you don't want to take too much risk, but in today's current interest rate environment, "conservative" can mean low returns. An experienced fee-based advisor can help you determine the appropriate amount of risk for your personal situation.

Now that we are in our sixties, we are using a fairly conservative 60-40 allocation: 60% in short-term bonds and 40% in stocks that include exposure to large, small, growth and value, domestic and international companies, as well as some REIT exposure, with a small portion in emerging markets. Based on past experience, we have projected that these funds could last 40 to 50 years. Now, there are no guarantees, and we have made some assumptions, such as that the amount we need during our lifetime won't exceed a 5% withdrawal annually.

Of course, we have no idea what our son's needs will be 25 years from now. Nor do we know what the economic conditions are likely to be. We are also depending on income from a real estate holding to supplement our needs and our son's future needs.

Once you have started working with your financial advisor and agreed to the proper investment portfolio for your situation, it is important for you to meet on a regular basis. Your goals won't remain static over time — they'll change as your life changes. That's why it's important to regularly discuss your investment plan with your advisor to ensure that it always reflects where you are today and where you want to be in the future.

A good advisor will help you make the right decisions and keep you calm and focused on your larger goals when markets are volatile. Getting in and out of the market every time something negative happens is not the best way to grow your wealth.

Though I think we have done a good job planning and investing, you can never get away from those small, nagging doubts.

Have we done all we can to ensure not only our own retirement, but that there will be sufficient assets to last another 50 years or so for our son?

Amy's Journey

Nothing much keeps me up at night. I am so exhausted by bedtime, I sleep quite well.

While it is demanding and restricts my life significantly — and I am quite envious of those parents whose kids do move on — I have made peace with this path that I am walking, running, dancing. I have mostly found a balance between home, work and the tiny bit of free time that I take for myself.

Should I die before James, I have a life insurance policy in a special needs trust that should cover hiring someone to live with him and take care of him.

Although my daughter would step up to the plate, I don't want her to have to do that. And I have no other family or other support who would be willing to help.

James is 27 and does not have any postsecondary education and could not live alone. I'm not really sure yet if he could live with a roommate or in a group home; probably, but I'm still working on that.

Because James does not drive, transportation is one of our biggest challenges. He uses a local car service, and it's okay, but certainly not great. Otherwise, I drive him everywhere.

Employment for James is very challenging as well. He is overly confident and not respectful enough of authority (although I have very little problem with this personally). He also obsesses over food and has a hard time staying focused.

Right now, he is a volunteer at Goodwill, and I'm working to try to get him employed at Delicious Delights and/or Lowe's.

He does get some SSI/Social Security, which wouldn't even be enough to feed him for the month, let alone pay for his housing and all the other expenses in life.

Though it would be incredibly painful, like other parents of kids with special needs, I hope I outlive my child so that there is no need for someone else to provide for his care.

Conclusion

"No pessimist ever discovered the secret of the stars, or sailed to an uncharted land, or opened a new doorway for the human spirit."

– Helen Keller

Even after 40 years of relevant experience and insight from my career in investing/financial services, I am constantly wondering if I have done everything I can to ensure that our son is taken care of. Will he have all the resources he needs to have a good life when Mom and Dad are gone?

As I was finishing writing this book, I looked back at everything we'd done over the years to help our son. There it was, in black and white. And I realized for the first time that our son truly will be okay.

When we are gone, not only will he be taken care of, he also will have the means to lead a fulfilling life and not be a financial burden to our daughter or any other family member.

We're all on a journey with our children. I hope that by sharing my journey with you — and what wisdom I've gained along the way — you too can experience your own powerful realization one day and know with faith, humility and confidence that your child will be taken care of today, tomorrow and always.

Letter of Care

Prepared for:

[Full Name]

[Date]

[Child's Name]

[Note: This is a sample document. For a fillable Letter of Care, go to bit.ly/letter_of_care. For more information on how and when to use a Letter of Care, see pages 55 – 56.]

The Letter of Care template is provided courtesy of Charleston Investment Advisors, an independent wealth management firm located in Charleston, South Carolina.

A Path Forward

Introduction

Our goal is to ease the emotional and financial burden associated with caring for a loved one with special needs. The steps you must take can be difficult. They may even make you, or your loved one, uncomfortable. But taking these steps can have a profound impact on the quality of your loved one's life after you are gone. Creating a Letter of Care for your loved one with special needs is one such step — emotional and difficult, yet tremendously important.

The Letter of Care is designed to provide basic information about your loved one's personal, medical, legal, and financial needs to guardians, caregivers, relatives or friends — those responsible for providing physical, emotional and financial care when you are unable to do so. Like a map, it guides the caregivers through the day-to-day support your loved one requires.

More importantly, your hopes and desires are put into writing so that others will know your wishes for the future and be able to carry them out.

This is meant to be a living document, something that you should revisit from time to time when information changes or when milestones are met. The Letter of Care is not a legal document, but it should be signed and dated upon completion. Any updates should also be signed and dated. Once complete, please share your Letter of Care with the people who are most likely to provide care and have responsibility for your family member with special needs. You should also place a copy with other important documents, such as your will.

Letter of Care — Personal Note to Your Caregiver

Date:

Prepared for: Name:

DOB:

SS#:

Phone number:

E-mail

Dear Caregiver,

This is a letter of care for [Child's Name]. It is intended to provide basic information about his/her personal, medical, legal, and financial needs to guardians, caregivers, relatives or friends — people like yourself who have agreed to provide physical, emotional and/or financial care when we are unable to do so.

This Letter of Care is not a legal document, but a living expression of our hope, dreams and care for [Child's Name].

Very sincerely yours,

Table of Contents

Personal Information

[I/We] want to give a brief overview of [Name]'s life up to this point.

Provide an overview of the dreams and hopes you have for [Name] for the future.

Provide an overview of the fears you have for [Name] for the future.

Describe [Name]'s day-to-day life.

Our aspiration is that [Name] can do the following in the future:

We feel strongly that [Name] should be entitled to:

We hope that the following values will always be communicated and upheld to [Name]:

Full Name: _____

Nickname: _____

Social Security number: _____ Date of birth: _____

Address: _____

_____

Home phone number: _____ Cell phone number: _____

E-mail address: _____ Password: _____

Weight: _____ Height: _____ Shoe size: _____ Clothing sizes: _____

Gender: Male   Female

Race: _____ Religion: _____

Fluent language (s): _____

Country of citizenship: _____

If married, spouse's name: _____

Spouse's date of birth: _____

Children's name(s) and date(s) of birth:

_____

_____

_____

Personal Relationships

Mother's Name: _____

Address: _____

Phone number: _____ Social Security number: _____

E-mail address: _____ Birth date: _____

City and state where born: _____

Religion: _____ Race: _____

Blood type: _____

U.S. citizen: Yes   No

Marital status and date: _____

Name of spouse: _____

Father's Name: _____

Address: _____

Phone number: _____ Social Security number: _____

E-mail address: _____ Birth date: _____

City and State where born: _____

Religion: _____ Race: _____

Blood type: _____

U.S. citizen: Yes   No

Marital status and date: _____

Name of spouse: _____

Aunt(s) and Uncle(s) — Mother's side:

Name:_____ Age: ____

Address: _____

Phone: _____ E-mail address: _____

Name:_____ Age: ____

Address: _____

Phone: _____ E-mail address: _____

Aunt(s) and Uncle(s) — Father's side:

Name:_____ Age: ____

Address: _____

Phone: _____ E-mail address: _____

Name:_____ Age: ____

Address: _____

Phone: _____ E-mail address: _____

Siblings:

Sibling Name: _____

Age:_____ Gender: Male Female

Address: _____

Phone: _____ E-mail address: _____

Sibling Name: _____

Age:_____ Gender: Male Female

Address: _____

Phone: _____ E-mail address: _____

Other Relatives & Friends:

Name:_____ Relationship: _____

Address: _____

Phone: _____ E-mail address: _____

Name:_____ Relationship: _____

Address: _____

Phone: _____ E-mail address: _____

Name:_____ Relationship: _____

Address: _____

Phone: _____ E-mail address: _____

Personal Preferences/Routines

A copy of Individual Habitation Plan attached: Yes   No

Favorite recreational activities include:

_____

_____

Likes to be with the following people when engaged in these activities:

_____

Interests and hobbies include:

_____

_____

Enjoys vacations such as:

_____

Needs an accessible hotel room: Yes   No

Likes to wear:

_____

_____

Favorite books include:

_____

_____

Favorite movies/TV shows include:

_____

_____

Favorite music includes:

_____

_____

Needs the following things and services in order to be safe and healthy:

_____

_____

Needs to avoid and be kept away from:

_____

_____

May exhibit the following behaviors:

_____

_____

These behaviors should be dealt with by:

_____

_____

Is upset by:

_____

_____

Is angered by:

_____

_____

Expresses anger by:

_____

_____

Is afraid of:

_____

_____

When upset or angry, the following helps him/her feel better:

_____

_____

_____

Weekday schedule includes:

_____

_____

_____

_____

Weekend schedule includes:

Calendar attached: Yes   No

_____

_____

_____

_____

Usually awakens around _____ AM and goes to sleep around _____ PM

Morning routine:

_____

_____

_____

Nighttime routine:

_____

_____

_____

Primary method of ambulation: _____

Primary method of communication: _____

Primary signs include:

_____

Needs help with (eating, drinking, brushing teeth, brushing hair, dressing, bathing, toileting, etc.):

_____

_____

Uses the following incontinence supplies: _____

_____

Living Arrangements

The best living situation for [Name] is (e.g., living with relatives, living with friends, living in a group home or institution in a shared room or a single room, etc.)**:**

First choice: _____

Second choice:_____

Third choice:_____

Current living arrangements:

_____

_____

Past living arrangements:

_____

_____

If living on his/her own, complete the following:

Address: _____

Title: _____

Mortgage: _____

Insurance: _____

Property Tax: _____

Mortgage Documents/Deed/Title:

Where kept (i.e., safety deposit box, file cabinet, etc.):

_____

Homeowner's Insurance Policy (Carrier's name): _____

Policy number: _____

Owner: _____ Insured: _____

Premium/frequency: _____

Agent's name: _____

Phone number(s): _____

Address: _____

_____

E-mail address: _____

Utilities: **Cable/Internet — Provider:** _____

Account: _____

Account holder: _____

Phone: _____

Billing address: _____

_____

Water — Provider: _____

Account: _____

Account holder: _____

Phone: _____

Billing address: _____

_____

Electricity — Provider: _____

Account: _____

Account holder: _____

Phone: _____

Billing address: _____

_____

Cell Phone — Provider: _____

Account: _____

Account holder: _____

Phone: _____

Billing address: _____

_____

Landline Phone — Provider: _____

Account: _____

Account holder: _____

Phone: _____

Billing address: _____

_____

Maintenance: Pest/Termite Control — Provider:

    Account: _____

    Account holder: _____

    Phone: _____

    Billing address: _____

    _____

Other (e.g., lawn, maid, etc.):

    Provider: _____

    Account: _____

    Account holder: _____

    Phone: _____

    Billing address: _____

    _____

    Provider: _____

    Account: _____

    Account holder: _____

    Phone: _____

    Billing address: _____

    _____

    Provider: _____

    Account: _____

    Account holder: _____

    Phone: _____

    Billing address: _____

    _____

Transportation

Can drive a car: Yes   No

Daily transportation needs: _____

      Car make: _____

      Car model: _____ Year: _____

      License plate #: _____

      Driver's license #: _____

      Expiration: _____

      AAA membership account number: _____

      AAA phone: _____

Auto insurance policy (Carrier's name): _____

Policy number: _____

Owner: _____ Insured: _____

Premium/frequency: _____

Agent's name: _____

Phone number(s): _____

Address: _____

_____

E-mail address: _____

School/Work

Currently Attends [level of school and type of school]:

_____

School name: _____

Address: _____

_____

Contact person: _____

Phone number(s): _____E-mail address: _____

Ages attended: _____Grade level completed: _____

Individual Education Plan (IEP) attached: Yes   No

Also attends the program(s) below:

Program: _____

Length of program: _____ Teacher's name: _____

Address: _____

_____

Phone number(s): _____E-mail address: _____

Program: _____

Length of program: _____ Teacher's name: _____

Address: _____

_____

Phone number(s): _____E-mail address: _____

Program: _____

Length of program: _____ Teacher's name: _____

Address: _____

_____

Phone number(s): _____E-mail address: _____

Previously attended:

School/program: _____

Length of program: _____ Teacher's name: _____

Address: _____

_____

Phone number(s): _____E-mail address: _____

School/program: _____

Length of program: _____ Teacher's name: _____

Address: _____

_____

Phone number(s): _____E-mail address: _____

Special academic abilities include:

_____

_____

Integrated into regular classes during his/her education: Yes   No

In the future, we hope that educational plans include:

_____

_____

Day Program:

Currently: attends a day program   has a job

_____

Describe: _____

_____

Location: _____

Work phone number: _____ Contact name: _____

Past programs or jobs that were not appropriate:

_____

The best day program or job for him/her would be: _____

Legal

Current Guardian: _____

Relationship: _____

Name: _____

Address: _____

_____

Phone number(s): _____

E-mail address: _____

Declared incompetent: Yes   No

Successor Guardian: _____

Relationship: _____

Address: _____

_____

Phone number(s): _____

E-mail address: _____

Name of Trust: _____ Date of trust: ____

Current Trustees:

Name: _____

Address: _____

_____

Phone number(s): _____

E-mail address: _____

Representative Payee:

The Representative Payee was appointed by the Social Security Administration to receive Social Security and/or Supplemental Security Income benefits for [name]. The Representative Payee's main responsibility is to use the benefits to pay for current and foreseeable needs of [name] and properly save any benefits not required to meet current needs.

Name: _____

Address: _____

_____

Phone number(s): _____

E-mail address: _____

Power of Attorney:

Name: _____

Address: _____

_____

Phone number(s): _____

E-mail address: _____

Date Power of Attorney was granted: _____

Wills:

Where kept (i.e., safety deposit box, file cabinet, etc.):

_____

Trusts:

Where kept (i.e., safety deposit box, file cabinet, etc.):

_____

Living Wills:

Where kept (i.e., safety deposit box, file cabinet, etc.):

_____

Durable Powers of Attorney:

Where kept (i.e., safety deposit box, file cabinet, etc.):

_____

Guardianship Order:

Where kept (i.e., safety deposit box, file cabinet, etc.):

_____

Income Tax Records:

Where kept (i.e., safety deposit box, file cabinet, etc.):

_____

_____

Funeral arrangements have been made: Yes   No

If "Yes," name of funeral home: _____

Address: _____

Phone number: _____ E-mail address: _____

Name of cemetery: _____

Address: _____

Phone number: _____ E-mail address: _____

Contact person: _____

Payments: have been made   have not been made

Service to be held: Yes   No

Monument/gravestone: Yes   No

    Buried or   Cremated

Final arrangements should include:

_____

_____

_____

Medical

Birth Information:

Weight: _____ Length: _____

Obstetrician name and address: _____

_____

City and state where born: _____

Hospital name and address: _____

_____

Information about the delivery: _____

Health Insurance:

Medical: _____

Policy number: _____

Premium/frequency: _____

Agent's name: _____

Phone number(s): _____

Dental: _____

Policy number: _____

Premium/frequency: _____

Agent's name: _____

Phone number(s): _____

Vision: _____

Policy number: _____

Premium/frequency: _____

Agent's name: _____

Phone number(s): _____

Other Health Insurance: _____

Policy number: _____

Premium/frequency: _____

Agent's name: _____

Phone number(s): _____

Diagnoses:

_____

_____

Diagnostic and genetic tests performed, including dates, doctor/laboratory performing tests and results:

_____

_____

Intellectual functioning level: _____

Vision level: _____

Contact lenses or glasses: _____

If contacts, brand and prescription: _____

Eye Doctor: _____

Vision prescription: _____

Hearing aid: Yes   No

Speech and communication: _____

Seizures: Yes   No

Blood type and conditions: _____

Primary Care Physician:

Name: _____

Address: _____

_____

Phone number(s): _____ E-mail address: _____

Are visits scheduled at specific times of year?   Yes   No

Specialist:

Name: _____

Address: _____

_____

Phone number(s): _____ E-mail address: _____

Are visits scheduled at specific times of year?   Yes   No

Dentist:

Name: _____

Address: _____

_____

Phone number(s): _____ E-mail address: _____

Are visits scheduled at specific times of year?   Yes   No

Orthodontist:

Name:_____

Address: _____

_____

Phone number(s): _____ E-mail address: _____

Are visits scheduled at specific times of year?   Yes   No

Nursing care: Yes   No

Nursing care required because:

_____

Care is given at home unless noted below.

Name of firm or facility: _____

Primary contact: _____

Name: _____

Address: _____

_____

Phone number(s): _____ E-mail address: _____

Allergies:

Allergic to: _____

Method of birth control: _____

Ambulatory: Yes   No

Medical equipment (e.g., wheelchair, adaptive cutlery, glasses, contact lenses, hearing aids, hand splints, orthotics, shower chair, accessible van, augmentative speech device, etc.):

_____

_____

Prescription Medication:

Name: _____

Dosage: _____

Reason for medication: _____

Prescribing doctor: _____

Over-the-counter medications and items:

_____

_____

_____

Needs help to take his/her medicine: Yes   No   Name of helper_____

Picks up/buys medicine: Yes   No

Helps him/her to take medicine at this time: _____

Can swallow pills: Yes   No

The best way to get him/her to take medicine is:

_____

_____

Diet is restricted as follows (e.g., no sugar, no salt, no foods that would present a choking hazard such as nuts or chewing gum, etc.):

_____

_____

Other: _____

_____

Please be aware of these additional medical conditions:

_____

_____

Financial

Needs help with banking: Yes   No

Name of Bank: _____

  Account holder: _____

  Account number: _____

  Type: _____

  Debit card: _____

  Web address: _____

  Online user name: _____

  Online password: _____

  Billing address: _____

  Statements: Online Only   Mailed

Name of Bank: _____

  Account holder: _____

  Account number: _____

  Type: _____

  Debit card: _____

  Web address: _____

  Phone number: _____

  Online user name: _____

  Online password: _____

  Billing address: _____

  Statements: Online Only   Mailed

Safety Deposit Box: _____

  Bank: _____

  Box holder: _____

  Where is key located? _____

Name of Credit Card Company: _____

    Account holder: _____

    Account number: _____

    Type: _____

    Card number: _____

    Web address: _____

    Phone number: _____

    Online user name: _____

    Online password: _____

    Billing address: _____

    Statements: Online Only   Mailed

Name of Brokerage Account Company: _____

    Account holder: _____

    Account number: _____

    Account type: _____

    Web address: _____

    Phone number: _____

    Online user name: _____

    Online password: _____

    Billing address: _____

    Statements: Online Only   Mailed

Financial Advisor:

Name: _____

Company name: _____

Address: _____

_____

Phone number(s): _____ E-mail address: _____

CPA:

Name: _____

Company name:_____

Address: _____

_____

Phone number(s): _____ E-mail address: _____

Can pay bills and stick to a budget: Yes   No

Finances are managed on a day-to-day basis by:

Name: _____

Address: _____

_____

Phone number(s): _____ E-mail address: _____

Relationship: _____

Person who is best able to help with personal finances is:

Name: _____

Address: _____

_____

Phone number(s): _____ E-mail address: _____

Relationship: _____

Receives an allowance: Yes   No

Allowance amount of $_____ is paid weekly/monthly/quarterly by: _____

[Name] or his/her Representative Payee receives the following government benefits (e.g., Social Security, SSDI, SSI, etc.):

Service/benefit: _____

Frequency: _____ Amount: _____

Monthly bill schedule attached: Yes   No

Federal/State/Community Benefits:

Service/benefit: _____

Provider: _____

Start date: _____ End date: _____

Service/benefit: _____

Provider: _____

Start date: _____ End date: _____

Life Insurance Policy (Carrier's name): _____

Policy number: _____

Owner: _____ Insured: _____

Premium/frequency: _____

Agent's name: _____

Phone number(s): _____

Address: _____

_____

E-mail Address: _____

About the Authors

Donald A. Bailey

A lifelong South Carolinian, Donald began his career in the insurance industry with a focus on financial planning. After working as a financial planner for E. F. Hutton, he founded Donald Bailey & Associates in order to offer independent advice and holistic planning to his clients.

Donald is committed to community involvement, having served on the Board of Trustees at the University of South Carolina (USC) and most recently founding The College Transition Connection, Inc., a non-profit organization whose mission is to help South Carolina colleges create post-secondary programs for young adults who may have an intellectual disability.

Donald holds a degree in Marketing from USC. He and his wife Caroline have two children and three grandchildren and reside in Mt. Pleasant, South Carolina.

J. William G. Chettle

William Chettle is a Vice President of Marketing with Loring Ward. William has two decades of financial services experience, including senior positions in National Sales, Communications and Marketing at Prudential Securities and Wachovia Securities.

William has an M.F.A. in film-making from New York University and graduated summa cum laude and Phi Beta Kappa from Harvard with an A.B. in English and American Literature and Language. He and his wife, along with their two cats and 8,000 books, live in Washington, D.C.

Acknowledgments

It took the ideas, hard work and inspiration of many people to create this book. We want to thank Don's wife Caroline, Stephanie Lee and the other families who shared their stories, Meg Grigal, Madeleine Will, Tony Plotner from the University of South Carolina, Joe Ryan at Clemson University, Cindi May at The College of Charleston, Deb Leach from Winthrop University, Stephanie Mackara and Erica Smith from Charleston Investment Advisors, Harris Pastides and Susan Flynn at Coastal Carolina. We also want to thank a number of people at Loring Ward who helped make this book possible, including Alex Potts and Mike Clinton for their friendship and support, Kate Tengberg, who brought her creative talents to the layout and cover design, and Karen Parker for her editing expertise. Finally, we want to thank Don's son Donald for helping his family and friends better understand the life of an individual with a disability.